Wimp or gladiator

Contradictions in acquiring masculine sexuality

**Janet Holland, Caroline Ramazanoglu
Sue Sharpe**

WRAP/MRAP PAPER 9

the Tufnell Press

Published by
the Tufnell Press,
47 Dalmeny Road,
London, N7 0DY
England

First published January, 1993

British Library Cataloguing-in-Publication Data
A catalogue record for this book is
available from the British Library

ISBN 1 872767 90 7

Printed in England by Da Costa Print, London.

CONTENTS

vi

Sexuality is a central site in men's struggles to become masculine.[1] The cultural ideal of western masculinity produces some men as virile, romantic, successful and powerful, but only in relation to others who are not. Western sexuality is characteristically competitive, aggressive and centres on men's desires and men's demonstration of potency. Heterosexual young men embark on sexual activities with women in social situations in which they must strive to become victorious gladiators in the sexual arena, while avoiding the many pitfalls which can reduce them to the ignominy of being a wimp, a failed man, a sexual flop.

Recognition of the power of heterosexual masculinity has, in recent years, been supported by a growing area of studies of masculinity by men (Ramazanoglu 1992). The feminist perspective which informs much of this research has the effect of problematising men's heterosexual behaviour. As Arthur Brittan (1989: 204) has pointed out, masculinity as a topic did not exist prior to the feminist challenge to male power, since heterosexual men have not conventionally seen themselves as a problem. These studies very generally identify masculinity as socially constructed, as something which men achieve rather than are born with (Tolson 1977; Brod 1987; Kimmel 1987; Chapman and Rutherford 1988; Clatterbaugh 1990; Hearn and Morgan 1990; Seidler 1989, 1991; Segal 1990).

Morgan (1981) proposes that masculinity is not uniform since there are various versions which men 'do' in different ways, differentiated by sexual identity, class, ethnic and other structural and cultural differences. Carrigan, Connell and Lee (1985) suggest that rather than men conforming to one monolithic version of masculinity, western cultures produce a dominant or hegemonic masculinity constructed in the image of the white, middle class male and differentiated from subordinated masculinities (see also Wight, 1992; Wood 1987; Nix *et al.* 1988). The idealised conception of the 'real man' pressures young men to differentiate themselves from gay men, women and failures.

The considerable power that is invested in masculinity means that part of being a 'normal' man is the exercise of power over women. Lesbians challenge and undermine 'normal' masculinity, since they can define their own versions of femininity without the need for dependence on men for sexual satisfaction.

Homosexual men undermine masculinity because they do not need to dominate women or head families; they can be socially 'weak' and yet sexually successful. The dominant cultural images of lesbians and gay men are, therefore, extremely negative, and reinforced with discriminatory practices and violence. Any women who appears not to desire a particular man can be derided as frigid, inadequate, lacking, unfulfilled. Gay men are deviant, failed men, justly punished by the scourge of AIDS. The virulence of homophobia and the well-documented violence of men towards women might be taken to indicate, however, that the certainties and satisfactions of heterosexual masculinity are more complex than might appear.

Heterosexual men are vulnerable in three main respects. First, they may simply fail to measure up to their gender; they may not be able to attract a female partner or achieve intercourse. Since men are born into male bodies, but not into the successful accomplishment of culturally appropriate versions of masculinity, becoming a man is a complex process of learning and doing within shifting sets of social constraints. Young men entering into their first sexual encounters and relationships have both to initiate contact, and to confront the possibility of failure. (While women may well make sexual advances to young men, such advances are culturally unfeminine and so potentially undermine the success of his manhood.) Spotty youths not fancied by the girls, boys who lack social skills or confidence, whose sexual technique appears to them inept, who lack knowledge of women's bodies and feelings, risk their manhood. Fear of failure to achieve masculinity is a fear of lack of potency both personally and socially (Tiefer 1987). It encourages resistance through subcultural variants of masculinity and also boasting of exploits, aggression, competition, homophobia, racism and the general subordination of women, as young men set out to prove themselves.

Second, young men are vulnerable, as Seidler (1989) has argued, because negotiating sexual encounters can engage their emotions, connect them to their need for affection, and render visible their dependence on women. This can evoke in them the desire for the female, symbolised by the mother, against which masculinity is socially constructed. Wendy Hollway (1984: 66) says that while men do have sexual power, satisfying their 'sex drive' puts them at risk of forming a relationship.[2] Falling in love makes them vulnerable. Their aim of demonstrating their masculinity exposes young men to very direct pressures to succeed sexually within a very constraining definition of sexual intercourse. Men experience vulnerability not primarily through social inequalities between partners, but through the development of caring, tenderness, the exposure of their own emotional desires, which attach them to particular women in particular relationships (Hall 1991). Successful masculinity puts them under pressure to conceal the extent of their vulnerability through caring, dependency, loving and any other characteristic of nurturing or effeminacy. A man laid low by love can be dependent, hurt, dismissed, rejected; he is a man at risk as a man.

Third, men are vulnerable when they enter into sexual relationships with women, because women do not necessarily conform to cultural ideas of subordinated femininity. Research on young women's sexuality has produced complex accounts of young women's struggles both to be feminine and to resist the cultural imposition of femininity. Their negotiations of heterosexual encounters appear to be complex processes in which being successfully feminine potentially subordinates them to men, robs them of their own desires and puts them at risk of pregnancy, disease, or intimate violence (Holland *et al.* 1992a; Thompson 1990; Kent 1990; Aggleton 1992; Wight 1990.) In order to succeed sexually, young men need to gain access to a woman, penetrate her vagina and achieve their own orgasm. As Wendy Hollway has put it (1981; 39) '... men measure their masculinity against women's sexuality'. Where women develop their own desires, or resist subordination, their sexuality, the material reality of their bodies and desires, constitute a potential threat to conventional masculinity.

As young men struggle to produce themselves as masculine, they are drawn into the exercise of power over women, but simultaneously exposed to the possibilities of failure. In this paper we explore young men's strategies for defending themselves against vulnerability, and show how becoming successfully masculine pressures young men into sexual strategies which are also mechanisms for subordinating women. This analysis is based on empirical studies described in the following section.

Sexuality and young people: The WRAP/MRAP studies

The Women, Risk and AIDS Project (WRAP) and Men, Risk and AIDS project (MRAP) research teams have generated a large body of qualitative data on the sexual knowledge and practice of young men and women in two studies undertaken since 1988. The first study was of the accounts of their negotiation of sexual encounters given by young women aged 16-21 in London and Manchester.[3] The Men Risk and AIDS Project (MRAP) was a comparative study of 46 young men in London between 1991 and 1992.[4] (See Appendix 1 for a brief statistical description of the two samples.)

We aimed in these two studies to build up a detailed picture of the sexual practices, beliefs and understanding of young people to document and interpret their understanding of HIV and sexually transmitted diseases; their conceptions of risk and danger in sexual activity; their approaches to relationships and responsibility within them, and their ability to communicate effectively their ideas on safety within sexual relationships. It is also our intention to contribute to the development of the theory of the social construction of sexuality, by identifying some of the complexity of the processes and mechanisms through which young people construct, experience and define their sexuality and sexual practices.

The tensions between young men's sexual power and their vulnerability do much to complicate strategies for achieving safer sex (see also Pleck *et al.*1988; Ingham *et al.* 1991; Wight 1992). A real man should please a women sexually and satisfy his non-sexual desires for company, nurturing, care and reproduction. But negotiating mutual pleasure and safety depends on effective communication about needs and desires. This level of communication runs counter to the pull of conventional masculinity and femininity (see also Kent *et al.* 1990; Wight 1992; Woodcock *et al.* 1992).

A clear distinction between sex and love was identified by the young women in our earlier study, but on the whole the young women worked hard at integrating the two. Maintaining a distinction between 'fucking' and 'making love', however, was central to much of the young men's discussion of sexuality. In the interview excerpts used in this paper it is striking that the young men very generally take their partners to have been sexually satisfied, whereas the accounts given by young women in our previous study indicate both much lower levels of satisfaction, and young women's efforts to conceal their lack of pleasure from their partners (Holland *et al.* 1992b). Concern with sexual risk and safety is then only one of many pressures in the pursuit of intercourse and sexual relationships (see also Spencer 1984). Comparison between the accounts of their sexuality given by young men and young women indicates something of the complexity young men face in becoming masculine.

In this paper we draw on data primarily from the Men, Risk and AIDS Project (MRAP), referring where appropriate to the earlier study of young women. The analysis and interpretation of the data on young women feeds into and illuminates the work on young men. We use young men's accounts of their sexuality to explore what it means to argue that heterosexual young men are vulnerable in sexual relationships. This exploration is situated within an understanding that men generally exercise power over women, and that this power is strongly institutionalised in cultural constructions of masculinity.[5] These two studies suggest that men exercise considerable power in their pursuit of successful masculinity, without necessarily intending or consciously wishing to do so, and in spite of their persistent vulnerability.

A number of strategies which potentially reinforce male power are available to divert this vulnerability. These strategies include:

    (i)   adopting the protective coloration of the peer group;

(ii) objectifying and dismissing women in general, and in particular the woman who is the means by which first penetrative sexual experience is acquired (Litewka, 1977);

(iii) seeking out the knowing older woman from whom to acquire appropriate knowledge. These strategies will be discussed in more detail below.

(iv) wielding the weapon of attributing a negative sexual reputation to a woman;

These strategies will be discussed in more detail below, but first we examine some processes in men learning about sex. The process of learning about sex in whatever contexts was a crucial component in the construction of femininity, and their understanding of sex and sexuality, for the young women in the WRAP study (Thomson and Scott 1992). The way in which young men learned about sex provides a similar insight into their understanding and experience of masculinity.

THE KNOWING MAN: FORMAL AND INFORMAL SEX EDUCATION

(i) Learning about sex

Many of the young men we spoke to were unable to pin down exactly where or when they learned about sex, or certain aspects of sex and sexuality:

A: It's like saying where did you learn the alphabet or whatever, or homework, just everywhere I suppose. I don't think you can single particular places out as sources.   [YM 1][6]

A: I think I've always known what would go on in sex. Somebody didn't tell me one day and it was a revelation. I think I've always known from a very early age.   [YM 2]

A: I don't even know where I picked all that stuff up, but you just do, you know what I mean. When you are at school and that, you just like - things float about and not being taught at school and not being taught by your Mum and Dad, everybody kind of knows.   [YM 3]

A: Whether it came from books, parents or school, is kind of all mixed up, lost, it's all a long time ago.   [YM 4]

These comments illustrate a general perception prevalent among the young men that they 'just knew' about sex. This could be coupled with the acknowledgement of particular lacunae in their information. This perception speaks not so much of what were or were not seen as sources of sexual information, as of an ideological stance which is related to men as holders and creators of knowledge - the male as the norm. More specifically it is the male construction and definition of heterosexual sex - vaginal penetration, with the man as prime mover and actor - which is the norm. The assumption that men have knowledge can be disempowering for the individual young man who may in fact *not* know, but at a certain age cannot reveal that lack because he feels he is expected to know.

Our data supports the view that young men receive less formal sex education than young women (Allen, 1987; Currie, 1990). They frequently find the information provided by friends inaccurate and by parents and school irrelevant. Sixty-seven per cent of the young men found school sex education inadequate, 55 per cent had the same view of the sex education they received at home, and 51 per cent saw information from peers as inadequate or misleading. Young women in the WRAP sample were slightly less dismissive of school and home (63%; 47% respectively thinking sex education from these sources inadequate), but far fewer thought ill of the information acquired from friends (29% thought it inadequate or misleading).

Pornography in magazines and videos was a source of sex education mentioned frequently by young men and rarely by young women. While some of the young women did mention the experience of watching porn videos, in groups or with their boyfriends, they did not refer to them as a source of information or knowledge about sex or sexuality. Young men regarded them as a source of information about the female body.

Friends are mentioned as a source of information by many of the young men interviewed, but when they reflected on this, far fewer saw friends as a source of usable information. The more common response was to see talk about sex amongst friends as joking6, dirty language, boasting, and being one of the boys (see below). For some it gave rise to misinformation and mystification, and in some cases parents had to "put right" "schoolboy playground chat".

A: I was masturbating when I was about eleven and it was probably from there you got sort of the schoolboy playground chat about things. Then I used to come home and sort of come out with these things and mum would just burst out laughing and explain them to me properly.   [YM 5]

This young man also recognised his need to be "put right" at a later stage in what he had learned from friends and pornography:

A: But it was my parents, or my mother and my sister, my father who sort
of clarified it and said that it's not like that at all, don't think it's just like
dirty films and you know, horrible disgustingness like that, it's not like
that. I came home with one point of view from friends and watching films
and my parents gave me the other point of view.   [YM 5]

Some young men were able to talk to their mothers, or to mothers and
fathers about different aspects of sexuality and sexual practice:

A: There are certain ways you can talk to your mum and certain ways you
can talk to your dad, it it's like advice from a man, another bloke, yes, I
will go and talk to my dad obviously, but if it's more in the direction of
how women feel then its talking to my mum, isn't it?   [YM 1]

Others had been "sat down and given a lecture", although this could be
too late: "By the time I suppose my dad had plucked up courage to tell
me, I was sort of telling him what he was going to say next"   [YM 7]

But for many the subject was taboo, difficult to approach and embarrassing
"I think it's harder to talk to parents than it is to a stranger" [YM 25]. Others had
received minimalist information, often in a joking context, with the admonition
to 'be careful' and 'use something/a condom': "Don't do anything stupid, and
wear protection if you are going to...That was about it really." [YM 20] The relative
absence of instruction from parents, their acceptance of male sexuality and
young men 'going their own way', albeit with care, affords freedom from control.
This contrasts with the protective discourse and context of surveillance within
which young women learn about sex at home and in school (Thomson and Scott,
1991).

Other family members, older brothers and sisters, sometimes helped the
learning process, but this too could be joking and even derogatory as in "Got
your rocks off yet boy?" from an older brother.

Severe criticism of the inadequacy of school sex education was general from
both young women and young men, but the latter were more vehement. They
dismissed the scientific model: "Latin names and mechanics", "useless", "rubbish",
"completely irrelevant, nothing to do with sex", "OK if you were a monkey", and
saw the emphasis on reproduction as misleading. "I thought that every time you
had sex you definitely got pregnant unless you were protected, because they told
you the sperm goes up here and it fertilises the egg, and that's what happens!"
[YM 8]. If they had sex education when young, it provided an opportunity to
giggle at the rude words and embarrass the teachers; if they were older it was
too late:

A: In the first year they like didn't say much because everyone was sort of really childish, we didn't really learn anything, it was really embarrassing. In the fourth year everybody knew everything by then. What's the point?

[YM 9]

A: Nobody took it seriously, they told us things we already knew, they never told us like - they never ever told us how AIDS can be contracted sort of thing, they never told us anything like that, they just told us the basic mickey mouse stuff, like where the penis goes in, everyone knew that already so it didn't really help. [YM 10]

We conclude from our studies then that young men seem to receive less sex education compared with young women, and more of them consider that the information they do receive is inadequate or too late. But, as we have seen in the above discussion, there are three crucial interrelated differences in the overall context in which men and women learn about sex and their own sexuality: (i) the male is regarded as the knowing sexual agent and the actor; the woman is unknowing and the acted upon; (ii) 'normal' heterosexual sex is defined by an act which is seen as meeting male need and desire, and providing pleasure and satisfaction for the male; women are seen as gaining satisfaction from meeting men's needs; (iii) women learn about sex through a 'protective discourse' which emphasises their reproductive capacity and danger, particularly of unwanted pregnancy, and in which images of positive female sexuality, desire and pleasure are largely absent (Thomson and Scott, 1991).

Young men in our sample expected, and felt that they were expected, both to want to have sex (regarded as vaginal intercourse with male ejaculation) and to enjoy it. They were offered a positive male sexual identity, and this 'active' construction of masculine sexuality is predicated on a corresponding 'passive' construction of female sexuality in which any autonomous female desire is absent. The general background of a positive, active, knowing, pleasurable male sexuality as the norm, and the expectations which flow from it, can both create problems in practice when young men begin to have sexual experiences, and provide a shield and defence against 'failure'. It can create problems when practice falls short of expectations, particularly where female sexuality proves to be demanding and complex. It can provide protection from female sexuality through legitimation of the collective male strategies used to divert vulnerability, principally in the objectification and denigration of women.

(ii) Experience

Theory disrupted in practice

While many of the young men might have been able to present themselves as sexually knowledgeable, and so not needing to be taught about sex, putting theory into practice could reveal some of the contradictions in their sexuality.[8] One young man asserted that most sexual knowledge which is acquired:

> A: on hearsay is a load of crap ... it's a load of old rubbish, and it's not until you actually sort of, you're in, that you fling yourself in and you find out for yourself what happens, what she is going through and what you are going through. I felt I grew up a hell of a lot.   [YM 7]

He is alluding here to the processes by which sexual experience modifies sexual knowledge and understanding. Young men could encounter particular problems with putting the theory into practice when they had their first experience of sexual intercourse:

> A: I kind of knew all the background info, kind of I knew all the theory, if you know what I mean, but I hadn't done any of the practice.   [YM 11]

One young man had worried about the physical practicalities of it before, just as when younger, what to do about noses and teeth were seen as a problem before attempting the first kiss:

> A: I'd thought before, you know - well alright, I'm supposed to get on top, I understand that bit, but am I supposed to have my hands like this or my elbows or .. down like this and up like this, or - how am I supposed to, you know, the logistics of it.   [YM 12]

In the event he considered that his first experience of sexual intercourse went quite smoothly

> A: when it happened it just sort of get - you just do it without really thinking about it ... at the time it was completely, it just sort of flowed."

For him kissing had, in fact, been a harder technique to handle:

> A: But - I thought kissing was harder than sex actually. You know, the idea of it, like trying to work out what you do, but as soon as that came it

was easy enough."

For another the gap between theory and practice was wider, "it was a hit and miss affair" but things improved with practice, as was the comment of a number of the young men:

A: I thought I knew how I could handle it in my head and it was the practice that I couldn't sort of ... I knew what to do and I knew how to do it, and sort of emotionally I was ready, willing and able, but I think in actual practice I don't know, I suppose it was because I always sort of imagined how it would be and how to sort of act and how sort of to treat other people and how I would be treated, it didn't quite live up to that. But after the first time the second time was better and the third time was better, because I became more aware of what I was doing and how to do it.   [YM 5]

Young women were concerned about first sex, but the conventional model of the knowing, acting male, meant that they could expect the male to take responsibility for the technicalities. Young men, having achieved vaginal penetration and their own orgasm at the first attempt tended to feel that their mission had been successfully accomplished. Young women much more frequently expressed shock or disappointment at the pain or abruptness of the experience, compared with their more romantic expectations of a sexual relationship. One young woman, experienced herself, explicitly deferred to the knowing male:

Q: There is a lot of talk about sex, but not much about how you actually 'do' sex. Was that something that worried you?
A: Yeah, and 'how do I do it?' and 'what role do I have?'. I still am I suppose. Because I've only slept with, is it five? Six people? I still don't know whether I am doing it right, do you know what I mean? Lie back and think of England; I mean I do sometimes. I think it helps, do you know what I mean? I don't know what to do or anything.
Q: Would you like to do more?
A: I'd like experience, yeah, I'd definitely like experience. I'd like someone actually tell me whether I'm doing it right or wrong. [YW 14, Thomson and Scott, 1991]

Trial and error, learning together

Acknowledging inexperience and sharing the learning process with a partner can reduce the fear of failure, and the potentially threatening nature of the first sexual experience. Such caring relationships with young women are not available within the framework of many male peer cultures. The possibility of such a relationship, available only to some[9] young men, clearly eliminates the need for the more stringent self protective strategies of objectification and denigration of women. Several of the young men were in ongoing, caring relationships which had become sexual, and in many cases both partners had been virgins. Being able to laugh with each other about what was happening often eased couples through the experience. These types of description of first sex were also found in the young women's sample. Here is an example from a young man's description.

> A: We used to stay the night at each other's houses a lot. And it just happened like. You know, you get undressed and you're in the same bed. [YM 8]

In this case the young man had discussed sex and contraception with his partner and they used condoms. As far as the sex was concerned:

> A: Obviously it's kind of a bit difficult at first 'cos you're not really quite sure what to do, but it was alright after a while. .... We were both quite open about it - I mean I thought that the first time I'd have to like - if I - if it was going wrong I might be really embarrassed or something. I pretended it wasn't. But it was alright. I mean it's a laugh, it's just like - just burst out laughing sometimes. It's so ridiculous, you know, it's completely surreal, strange.

Another young man commented:

> A: It was funny. I mean you've got to get rid of your embarrassment and you're both in the same boat, you both know and it's just a laugh isn't it. I didn't find it a nerve-wracking experience like a lot of people do. I just sort of took it as it comes. If it doesn't work out the first time then you have another go. You laugh about it.   [YM 3]

A third couple had been 'going out' for about two months before the opportunity had arisen, but:

> A: I think basically we knew it was going to happen.   [YM 13]

In the event they found themselves alone in his parents' flat, found condoms in his sister's drawer and it was:

A: Quite enjoyable, I would say it get better as it goes along. I was a bit nervous about it.

Another virginal couple had discussed having sex, and the opportunity arose when they were babysitting for her little brother "...it just went on from there". He was afraid of a lot of things, whether she would get pregnant, whether he would be able to do it. But in the event on his report they both enjoyed it. Many of the young men assumed or inferred that women had enjoyed both first and subsequent sexual experiences with them, although few put this to the test of enquiry. From the young women's accounts, their experience of first sex was rarely enjoyable, and generally pleasure and desire were concepts somewhat lacking in their reports of their sexual experiences (Holland *et al.*, 1992a).

BECOMING MASCULINE

(i) The pleasures and perils of the peer group

Support through the vicissitudes on the road to masculinity might be sought by young men from their peers, but this process is complex, and fraught with tensions and contradiction. We attempt to tease out some of these in the following sections.

(a) Affirming male power: competition and vulnerability

When young men talk amongst themselves about their sexual exploits and experiences, they are not primarily seeking to gain knowledge about sex and sexuality, but attempting to create and reproduce a certain image of themselves. In this competition to demonstrate acceptable masculinity, to prove themselves as men, the image they must present is of a macho, knowing, and experienced male.

It might seem reasonable to assume that young men talk together in groups to express camaraderie and gain support. It appears from the accounts of the young men in this study and the work of Wight (1992), that such talk can be very unsupportive for the individual. In these groups, young men are subjected to teasing, having the mickey taken, and forms of collective pressure to express and define themselves in a particular way in order to prove their manhood. Aggression too can be seen in the negative labelling of those who fall short, or whose sexual claims are not believed - "wimps", "wallies" and "wankers". What the group does seem to support is a particular concept of hegemonic heterosexual masculinity, and separation from effeminacy, or homosexuality.

Some young men in the study felt that they could reject or had rejected the pressures of these male groups and their expression in male talk, often recognising them as unsupportive and a cover for the uncertainty experienced by their members:

A: I've never had outside pressures from friends when it comes to relationships. And if I did then they probably wouldn't be my friends anyway. ... It was more at college and then people didn't - or the people I went around with - didn't boast or stuff like that. There were a few odd people, but, you know, you knew they had.   [YM 3]

A: They used to go on about it - I've done it here, I've done it there, and I used to avoid that all the time, it didn't really bother me. I used to keep out of that sort of thing but I didn't used to say things like that because it wasn't true and everybody else knew they were lying as well so I don't see any point in it, a bit ridiculous really. I just used to ignore that sort of thing.
Q: Because everyone is giving their own bravado?
A: And everyone is giving their own rubbish, in the end they still come out with it as well, basically to be part of the crowd.   [YM 14]

For others, who are less confident, as we can see from this young man's assessment, it can be very important to be part of a group and to conform to expectations, however personally painful this process can prove to be. These types of groupings and the pressures they exert can be more prevalent and harder to resist in some social environments compared with others - in school, college and some work situations for example. A similar pattern can be observed in group pressures on young women to conform to a particular model of feminine sexuality through the use of threats to reputation (Mahoney, 1985; Lees, 1986).

Talk in groups can be perceived as positive from the male perspective when it provides a relatively public forum to demonstrate individual progress towards masculinity, to gain status and a shared sense of potential ownership or conquest of women. Having sex with a woman also removes power from women:

A: We talked about it but I didn't really learn anything. I mean when you're about fourteen you're completely sex starved, that's all you talk about.

Q: What kind of things do you talk about?
A: Just say "Whorr" an' that. Don't really talk about cervixes and...   [YM 8]

"Whorr!" here expresses these implications: it is an affirmation of manhood and masculinity expressed in the most crude physically sexual terms, and its use constructs women as powerless sexual objects to be fucked.

Competition in one form or another plays an integral role in the acquisition of masculinity, and several of these young men referred to a competition to lose their virginity:

A: ...there was a group of four of us, really, really close friends and I was like the first person to lose my virginity out of them. I think they were shocked because I had lost my virginity and they hadn't, like I think everyone had the idea that they would lose theirs first and it was like they...I don't know, I think that was partly why I wanted to do it as well, like it was a competition.   [YM 9]

The competitive pressure continues as the sexual career progresses:

A: ...it's a big image problem everyone's got with sex. It's got to be high, you have got to have sex all the time, sleep with loads of different girls, it's like that.
Q: Yes, and do you think guys still feel that way?
A: I think it is a bit of a competition all the time.   [YM 9]

For young men, success in this competition is sexual conquest, and the audience for this victory is the male peer group rather than the sexual partner:

Q: Do you think that sex means something different for the boys and for the girls?
A: Yes, definitely, men just see it as something that has got to be done, that's what I think, so your friends don't tease you. Women see it as something that really means something to them. We are using them to get something, I don't know, it's all ego when it comes down to it for the men ... it's like an achievement.   [YM 15]

For young women the situation is more complicated, for they must tread the treacherous line between losing their reputation through allowing sexual access to them, and the desired social status conferred by 'having a boyfriend' where sex is part of the relationship. When men are known for their sexual prowess it is seen as a gain in reputation, if women are known for their sexual activity, it is seen as a loss in reputation.

(b) Performance stories and striving for masculinity

Although there is some awareness among young men of the need to keep within certain parameters of credibility, the content of male talk about their sexual activities need bear little relation to their experience. There is a common acceptance of exaggeration and even lying, which is not necessarily publicly challenged, although it can contribute to a reputation as wally or wanker, or as in this case, an idiot:

> A: When you've got a gathering in a mate's house, and then it comes round to me - "What did you do?" and I say "I had sex, so what." They say have you done this, and do you fancy this girl, you know what I mean. They do my head in, I don't really mix with them now.
> Q: And do people tell the truth...
> A: Most of them lie, most of them anyway.
> Q: What, to give a good impression?
> A: I think they do. "Ah, I did it ten times last week" Everyone knows he's lying but he still says it, some people think he's a bloody idiot.   [YM 16]

Behind the boasting and exaggeration lies the dominant conception of heterosexual masculinity to which the young men aspire or from which they fear they may fall short. Acceptance and collusion can play a part in assessing the competition, and placing oneself in the performance.

> Q: And did you discuss that sort of thing a lot?
> A: Well, it all depends whether anybody had a girlfriend. If you had a girlfriend it was talked about, if you didn't you basically steered clear of the problem. I suppose it killed a lunchtime just talking about it. You often got the bloke who was making it up as he went along because he would contradict himself halfway through, but you still listened because he might know something that you don't know, and you are eager to find out what he does know.
> Q: Did you point out that he had made a contradiction and things like that?
> A: Basically we just let him finish and then we would take it with a pinch of salt whatever he said, some of it may be true, it may all be lies, but we just leave him, if that's what he wants to think there is no point in us breaking up his dreams or whatever. He went to the bother of telling us, we might as well leave him, if that's what he thought.

Q: Have you ever done that yourself?
A: I have got to admit I told one or two corkers a couple of times.
Basically you are always in the playground and everybody's there and
they have all got a story, and you are standing there and you have got no
story, so when it actually comes round to you, you decide to make up a
little bit, or if you have been out with a girl in the past, you just change
her name and change a couple of things about her so they think it's
somebody else, which works sometimes, but other times I had the feeling
they knew...   [YM 17]

But the performance stories of others can conflict with a young man's own
experience:

A: ...now I know he lied because he said "yes, yes, it was great", that was
like the first time he lost his virginity and I'm sure he was lying
because he was just saying how wonderful it was and I don't think
it is that wonderful. I think he was just saying that because
everyone presumes it is, everyone just presumes it's just the
best thing, it's not really.   [YM 9]

The reverse can also happen, when an actual sexual experience or
encounter can be seen by the young man as unbelievable to his friends,
so that he would hesitate to tell them for fear of being disbelieved, and
perhaps ridiculed. There are some examples in the section on sex with
an older woman below.

Performance stories function then to establish a young man's position in the
competition, and create and sustain a particular sexual image. Male fantasy and
bravado expressed in performance stories help to define the male model of
sexuality to which young men are expected to aspire:

Q: Tell me more about these sort of roles that are forced onto men. What
those may be in terms of having sex?
A: Well they tend to be rather crude. I was in a rugby club when I was
twelve or thirteen and the older rugby club members would go on about
sex. From the way they were talking you would get the impression that as
long as you were sticking your dick up somebody then you should be
happy and that was all there was to it. And you really didn't have to feel
anything for the person, in fact you shouldn't really feel anything for the
person at all.   [YM 18]

This succinct definition of the male model of sexuality identifies male power as sexual conquest over women and separation from emotional involvement with them. The male model operates as a defence against the vulnerability of involvement which we discuss further below, and creates vulnerability in the extent to which young men fall short of this ideal of male heterosexuality.[10] While some young men gave accounts of resistance to performance stories, these stories challenge as well as reinforce the acquisition of masculinity. Some young men characterised stories as boasting, exaggeration or lies. At least, the stories were assumed to be lies, otherwise the 'liar' would emerge as sexual superman and so victorious in the peer group competition. Performance stories undermine other men, while maintaining collective masculinity. Ridicule from one's peers serves as an instrument of control to ensure that the ideal of male heterosexuality is pursued.

(c) Gladiator or wimp: pressure and ridicule

The male group can exert pressure and employ ridicule, 'taking the mickey', to keep young men on the straight and narrow path towards heterosexual masculinity. A positive image is created by professing to have had sex with a girl, and even better, by having a 'good fuck' with a desirable girl. Imperfections in the woman would reflect on the man and lower his position in the male competition. The following young man speculates on his friends' critical response were he to present a less desirable girl as a conquest:

Q: Because blokes do tend to talk amongst themselves don't they? I don't know that it's very personal.
A: Yes. It's not personal, it's more like she was a good fuck you know, that's about it. She's got nice legs, nice tits, you know. It wouldn't be like - I don't think a guy could ever say to another guy that her breasts sagged you know and her legs weren't firm, you know what I mean?
Q: Why do you think you can't say it to blokes?
A: I think it's like a male dominant thing you know - "I just screwed a girl whose breasts were sagging, she had no arse, she was flat and everything." They would say "What! How could you do that in the first place?" That's what my friends would think.   [YM 19]

This young man went on to discuss the impossibility of revealing vulnerability and sexual failure to another man:

Q: But could you say, "I screwed this girl, she was absolutely great , but I

couldn't get anywhere." Could you ever say that?
A: No, I couldn't do that, not to another guy. He would say "What!"
Q: Whereas you are sure it has probably happened to him as well?
A: Yes exactly, but he would never admit to me, he could never say
Q: But why not, because women would admit it to one another?
A: I know. It's just the ... it's just the thing like ... it's like I think of it as all men are gladiators, right, and the more competitions they win with women, the more stronger they feel.   [YM 19]

The threat of sexual failure can turn a potential gladiator into a wimp. The following young man discusses in some detail the tensions and pain in having gained a reputation as a wimp, and the complex way in which the apparently joking attribution can act as a spur to performance:

Q: Why do boys want so much sex?
A: Maybe like because they have got friends that act this way like, they just want one thing and they like the idea really and they try to do it themselves and stuff like that, I mean they just copy each other really.
Q: So when you said earlier something about boys having a reputation, is that what you mean?
A: Yes.
Q: What their mates think of them?
A: Like supposing if they go to a party and meet a girl and nothing happens, then the guy's a wimp and stuff like that.
Q: Do you think their mates actually mean that or they just do it?
A: They do it to wind them up like
Q: But it still -
A: Yes, it still, like, hurts, it gets to your inside and like the person knows next time he has got to do it.
Q: It's funny, if when they call somebody a wimp they don't really mean it.
A: It's just really to give them a boost like. But the person who has been called that doesn't know what, sort of thing, but it just builds him up for the next time, he knows what to do.   [YM10]

This young man had indeed suffered from teasing from his friends, and when he eventually lost his virginity, it was more for their benefit than his own:

A: At the time I was at school - they used to say the only time you would get off with a girl if when she is deaf, blind and stuff like that and that's

where the feeling came from - "if only my friends could see me now."
Q: So you felt you had to prove yourself?
A: Yes.
Q: Why was that. Did you actually believe that they thought you were inadequate in some way?
A: Yes. Most of them take the mickey out of you and stuff like that and so you are more determined and so you feel you have to do it to prove yourself to them.
Q: But isn't it only a joke when they take the mickey out of you?
A: Most of the time it is, but it still hurts though, and it's just as bad as if they were serious.
Q: It's a funny thing to do to your friends isn't it?
A: Well it is and it isn't. Like most of them said it when I used to be at school like, one told me it's for your own good that people take the mickey out of you, the boy that told me was in the sixth form so he was much older, and he told me that, it's only for your own good and stuff like that. It makes you more determined to go out there and do it.

Young men facing failure in the eyes of their peers can redeem themselves by losing their virginity or gaining sexual access to a girl who can be passed off as desirable. Here a young man suggests that any failure in achieving intercourse can be admitted and in fact turned against their partner in male talk.

Q: Do you think that men actually feel afraid of the way they kind of perform? Afraid they might not be able to do it?
A: Yes, of course, definitely. Even when my friends are talking about it. Mostly they are scared of the flop, if they flop!
Q: And do they flop much?
A: I don't know anyone who has but they are scared of it.
Q: And would they admit it if they did?
A: Yes
Q: They would?
A: Yes to make everyone laugh.
Q: They wouldn't see it as some kind of failure?
A: It is failure but in the end it is just a joke you know because you have got a woman so excited that she wanted you. That's how everyone sees it as a joke. Not as sort of like you failed.
Q: Have you ever flopped?
A: No.
Q: Not ever?
A: No.   [YM 15]

This young man asserts that he could turn the experience of 'flopping' to his advantage in relating it to male friends, by transforming failure to maintain an erection into the power to arouse and then disappoint his partner, turning it into a joke at the woman's expense. For him this would avoid loss of sexual reputation.

These young men's accounts of their experiences of pressure, ridicule, the joking discourse (as either an attack on their masculinity or a means of defending it), suggest that a harsh dichotomy is being produced between the possibilities of becoming a wimp or a gladiator.

(ii) A hit and run affair: the 'bastard' syndrome

As we have seen from the discussion of male talk and the pressures from peers, one strategy used by men for dealing with the tensions and problems associated with losing their virginity is to adopt the 'male model' of heterosexuality. This is a way of exercising power and protecting oneself from vulnerability at the cost of a limited conception of sexuality. In the ideal typical form of the male model, as we have seen in a young man's description earlier, the woman is an object of male power and conquest, with no concern for her as a person, and the main objective is penetrative sex.[11] A number of young men in the study employed this approach for their first experience of sex. In this case it involves seeing loss of virginity as a one-off experience to be accomplished as soon and as speedily as possibly, a rite of passage with little concern for the woman.

Some of the young men continued to use this technique in their sexual relationships in general. There are several possible elements to the model as a way of sexual life. It can involve having one night stands - pushing women as far as you can towards penetrative sex, before they tell you to stop. A man can engage in short term affairs, 'love them and leave them', avoiding vulnerability by leaving the woman before she has a chance to engage his emotions or to leave him. This approach to sex and relationships may continue until perhaps they fall in love. One such young man was sorry that he had lost his virginity to someone for whom he did not care, when he would have preferred to have saved it for his current girlfriend, whom he loved:

A: It felt right at the time, just afterwards I felt well should I have done it or I don't know. I wish I had stayed a virgin until I met my current girlfriend".   [YM 20]

Another would have preferred to save it for someone special:

A: When I think back about it, I'm kind of upset that it wasn't someone more special to me because the first time is really supposed to be a big deal, or whatever. It was a big deal, I remember the feeling 'wow' afterwards, but it wasn't a really a good deal, it wasn't 'I'm in love' or whatever.   [YM 21]

But there were quite a number of young men in the sample for whom this self protective technique appeared to work, and they saw behaving in this way as an important part of masculine sexuality. In their view, who you had intercourse with, was less important for men than for women:

A: I think from a bloke's point of view they are not so bothered like who they lose their virginity to, or who they sleep with, and I think to a girl, or woman it means a lot more. [YM 9]

And another:

A: [Asked about whether he felt different on losing his virginity] I mean I think it is - I know it's a cliche but - I think it's a much bigger event in women's lives"   [YM 2]

This belief helped to boost their masculinity by distancing them from any feelings for the woman and concern for her feelings, in that if a woman was prepared to have sex after limited acquaintance, she fell short of the standard of ideal feminine sexuality.

Q: Was it her first time?
A: She said it was but I - I don't know whether it was or not. 'Cos like it was too quick like for her like, for a girl to say it was, like in a couple of hours. It would have been more if like if she was a virgin, so I reckon she wasn't.   [YM 22]

First sex was of course significant in a symbolic as well as practical sense, a rite of passage into manhood which made you 'one of the boys'. Some young men were very explicit about these aspects:

A: At the time I was thinking 'if only my mates could see me now' and stuff like that, and I must admit I didn't really think of the girl at the time. [YM10]

A: I thought to myself, I've got a right winner here, I've got something to

tell my mates now ... and you get really excited and everything because
you go to your mates and say yeah ... I was sweet. Had a result.   [YM 23]

A: It was sort of an achievement in a way. It felt good afterwards as well.
I never felt bad. I know it's funny saying it was an achievement because I
was going out to do it, but it was a main step in life, sort of thing.
Stepping out of one skin into another, if you are understanding me. Yes,
it was quite an important part of my life.   [YM 20]

The first time was the important one:

A: The second time was less important, because I had already done it you
know, so it didn't prove anything to me.   [YM 10]

Another explained:

A: I was 14 and dying to lose my virginity.   [YM 9]
A: Afterwards I was happy I had lost my virginity and I considered myself
a man or whatever.
Q: So it was just the once then, you both went your separate ways
never to see each other again?
A: Yes. I suppose at the time that's why I thought it was so great because
it wouldn't matter what happened like, if it took me longer, I wouldn't be
embarrassed because I wouldn't see her again, that's how I sort of felt. So
I thought it was good, because afterwards I thought that was it.

A number of the young men who adopted the 'bastard' approach to first sex
had met women on holiday, which provided them with a safe distance from the
women involved:

A: It was something that just happened to me, it was kind of someone I
met one night and that was it.   [YM 24]

This sense of emotional distance came through very directly in some of the
interviews:

A: It didn't really bother me at all. It's not as though you lose anything
really is it? It's just something in your mind, suddenly you know that
you're not a virgin any more.   [YM 23]

Others met their first sexual partners at parties and clubs, and in an extreme case the young man had only the word of his mates that he had managed it:

A: When I lost my virginity? Thirteen. It's a bit shameful, but I went out to a party and got kissed, and she was older than me, about seventeen ... I didn't even know the next day. Everyone just came round and said you lucky bastard, sitting there on your own. I can't remember a thing ... When you're pissed you don't know nothing. It's better off when it just happens, it just happens.   [YM 16]

The following young man had met some girls at a party, went off with his mate to their house. In this encounter he treats intercourse as something on which his performance can be measured:

A: It was weird really. I'd only known her a couple hours ... Like just went upstairs and stuff and it was just like straightaway, in a couple of hours
Q: And did you think that would happen?
A: I don't know. In a way, like from what my friends had told me... but I mean, I sort of took the chance really ...
Q: Did you enjoy it?
A: Yeah, it was quite a good experience. I thought I'd done alright like, never doing it before. I was quite pleased really   [YM 22]

Another picked up some girls at a club with his friend and it happened in the back of his friend's father's car:

A: We went to a club to meet some girls and met them and that was that really. There's not a lot I can say about that. It was fun, but it wasn't anything more serious, I've seen her, but I have never spoken to her since ... I saw her again but I never spoke to her again. I've no hang-ups about that.   [YM 21]

The 'hit and run' approach, reducing women to a subordinated 'other', is consistent with the pressures to lose virginity and compete in performance stories. It has more complicated ramifications when adopted as a way of life. The young man quoted above [YM 21] continued his sex life in a similar style, going for one night stands or short relationships, enjoying the chase more than anything else. He would then tire of the girl and move on. In his own report he has acquired the reputation of being uncaring, arrogant and hard, even amongst his friends. Keeping up the strategy of 'hit and run' could be a means of protecting against the vulnerability of caring, dependence and the risks of rejection.

The existence of the gladiatorial 'bastard' can make life even more difficult for the self confessed 'wimp'. One young man described the difficulties of being 'nice', he felt that women preferred 'bastard guys' since at least they asked women out. For 'bastard guys' rejection was not much of a problem, if one woman refused you just moved on and put your request to the next one. Nice guys found it difficult to approach women at all because more of their 'selves' were involved, and rejection was therefore harder to bear:

> A: most women seem to find sort of bastard guys attractive you know, the ones the ones that sleep around and - simply because they're the only ones that ever ask people out, you know, try and chat people up.
> Q: What, so you think the nicer guys lose out?
> A: Yeah I think they do. Simply because, I don't know, say, if you just go for a basic asking out you know, on a date, people who are more say, either romantic, or less interested in sex and more interested in a relationship have a lot at stake when they ask someone. You know, they've got all their emotional attributes at stake. You know, when they say - "look do you wanna go out Friday night?" They've got, you know "do you want to spend time with me? Do you like me as a person? Do you -?" you know, blah, blah, blah. Obviously "Do you find me attractive?, but "Do you like me?" Whereas the sort of bastard guys who are quite happy to sleep with anyone you know, if they say "Do you wanna go out tonight?" basically meaning you know, "Do you wanna go out for a drink - then we'll go back to my house, we'll have sex, we'll go away and we'll never talk to each other again. You know, they've go nothing to lose if someone says no, you know - "fine. How about you?" - they can just keep going on.   [YM 12]

Another 'nice' young man describes this problem from his own experience of wanting to approach a young woman whom he knew was waiting for him to do so since he had information from her friend to that effect:

> A: I mean I was not so much shy yes, but when it comes to actually making the move - I could talk to girls really casually, and have a right laugh with them, just as easy as I can with a bloke - but when it actually comes to THE sexual move, where it's like, if you like I mean it's the asking, whether it's by bodily asking or whatever, but actually asking I

always found really hard. I like really wanted to go out with this girl for a long time, since I started college, it was six months later when I actually asked her out. The thing is I knew she wanted to go out with me for that length of time as well. It's not just lack of confidence, it's not just thinking she is going to say no, it's not that that bothered me, I don't know what it is that bothers me. [YM 1]

Sexual success on the terms of the bastard syndrome does not necessarily render men invulnerable. In some cases, when 'the bastard syndrome' characterised a young man's sexual strategy, and women were successfully objectified, vulnerability could be revealed as providing the motor for such behaviour. One young man had been hurt by a girl for whom he did not particularly care, but who finished with him. After this experience he made sure that *he* was the one who decided to end relationships to protect himself from possible pain:

A: If a girl broke off a relationship with me then I would tend to be a little bit hurt, where I thought it was better if I broke it off with her, it wouldn't hurt so much. If I found another girlfriend pretty soon it would help me forget about it and it didn't hurt me as much" [YM 20]

He preferred to have short, sexual relationships

A: I was lucky because as I left one, it was only a matter of days or a week and I was into another relationship because I used to go out quite a lot then, clubs and that.

He did not care for any of these girlfriends, it was just something to do, slipping easily from one relationship to the next. He never really knew, or bothered to find out what the girls involved thought or felt, but he did manage to polish his technique by enquiring what they liked.

A: I tend to ask some girlfriends what they prefer sort of thing, and try and do that to them.
Q: And what do you find they do prefer?
A: A bit more caring and a bit more slowly, not just get undressed and do it and just sit there. They tend to like it a bit more caring and lovingly, even though I didn't love them. I did try to keep them happy.

But now he has been laid low, or perhaps raised up, by love. He is in love with his current girlfriend, has learned much from her:

> A: I'm more understanding towards women now, I'm less sexist as well for some reason, I don't know why ... It has changed me a lot, yes I've grown up another couple of years in the space of about five months. It's really helped me a lot.

Sex used just to be vaginal intercourse but now:

> A: When you are in a long term relationship you care about someone, you do want to make love, it feels different. It feels totally different. ... But now my girlfriend, because I love her and that, we can actually make love without actually having intercourse, just being nice to one another and that and just haven't got intercourse, but it feels we are making love. But with other girlfriends sex had to be intercourse, so it was sex.

This young man's experience illustrates the limits of the bastard syndrome. The pursuit of this model causes men to miss out on all areas of sexuality and desire which are more than intercourse, while ostensibly protecting them from vulnerability and pain. The syndrome demonstrates a direct exercise of male power, in which at the same time (as contributors to Seidler, 1991b have argued) men suffer from the limits of masculinity. Feminists have responded that this male pain is still consistent with men's exercise of power over women. The bastard syndrome can be a short phase at the beginning of a man's sexual career, be characteristic of periods interrupted by the pull of love or romance, or indeed become a way of life.

(iii) The knowing woman: Seduction and the older woman

We have seen that the sexually knowing man is the norm. The knowing woman can represent both threat and promise for young men on the route to heterosexual masculinity, and she appears in two of the strategies which can be used to divert vulnerability. The third strategy available to young men for ridding themselves of the burden of virginity, in the process recognising vulnerability, is to surrender to the superior knowledge and desire of the older woman. Here too the physical and emotional risks of sex or even a relationship with another virgin are being avoided. This surrender is simultaneously a conquest, and a consummation devoutly to be wished.[12] So much so that a number of the young men who had this experience either did not tell their mates because they assumed they would not be believed, or told them unbothered by disbelief because they were secure in their own knowledge and satisfaction. Holidays, one-off sexual encounters and short relationships characterised this type of virginity loss.

As with the bastard syndrome, a number of young men pursued the practice of seeking out older women in their sexual encounters and relationships, as their sexual career progressed. The age differences between themselves and their partners involved in the experiences reported by the young men in our sample ranged from one to seventeen years. In the latter case the young man had been in a pub and was invited back to a woman's room to help her with a repair problem. He felt that sex was something special which you needed to be old enough to appreciate, in his view a boy as young as 13 could not appreciate the experience. He was himself 15 at the time, and commented "I will remember that as long as I live"

> A: I went into the bedroom and she was naked on the bed. I went Um, my god!, because I kind of like froze, there was this woman, a good seventeen years my senior just sprawled out on the bed with nothing on. I had often seen the odd porno mag like and seen it, but when you actually see it really, you kind of go 'oh!' for the first time.   [YM 17]

He was not sure of her motivation, did she just want it or was she helping him out:

> A: but basically she just instructed me on what to do, and I had to do things ... she just talked me through it. It was really strange.

They had sex a couple of times, but he was exhausted and overwhelmed by the first night:

> A: It was a strange experience, I went round for the next four days with a great big smile on my face

> A: Me mum noticed the change as well. I just put it down to growing up.

> A: I told a couple of people, I told a couple of my mates at school after a little while, I thought sod it, I will, they can take the mick they don't have to believe me. I know within myself that I have actually done it, so if they don't believe me, they don't have to.

A night in a tent at the age of 14 with an older, experienced woman evoked similar fears of peer group ridicule for another young man:

A: I did talk to a few close friends about it, but the first time I didn't want to tell too many people because to say you lost your virginity to a girl on holiday in a tent it's just so unbelievable, like it's not worth it - everyone is going to turn round and go "oh yes?", so I kept that pretty quiet at the time, just like there was not point in saying, it sounds such a dodgy story. [YM 9]

One young man was desperate to lose his virginity - "I just wanted to get older so that I could have sex. Childhood wasn't very interesting actually". At 14 he had a two week holiday sexual relationship with a 19 year old:

A: I mean I couldn't have handled losing my virginity to another virgin because you wouldn't have a clue about what was going on, you know. So at least I've learned a few things, you know.   [YM 2]

Acknowledging superior knowledge in women was not always experienced unproblematically, and this young man was loath to abandon the idea of the sexually knowing male:

Q: So did she kind of teach you almost, show you what -
A: No, she didn't. I mean, you know it just, to a certain extent you know what to do by the time it comes. But obviously she did a bit of guiding, you know, But er, yeah, I wasn't totally ineffectual anyway.

For another young man there was a more explicit yielding to what he saw as the manipulation of slightly older women. In the first instance the woman chose him and

A: was pulling all the strings, while I was fairly binged throughout the whole thing ... I didn't really understand what was expected of me
                                                    [YM 18]

She became bored with him after a month "because I didn't really have the initiative, none at all". When it came to his first experience of 'coital sex', he was comforting a slightly older woman who was telling him of an intensely negative sexual experience, when:

A: she sort of dragged me off the bedroom and that was it. I didn't even know it was going to happen, right up until that point. It came upon me as quite a surprise.

Q: Was it something she was aware of what she wanted and you were less aware?

A: Yes, I think so, yes. I think I was quite manipulated looking back on it really. But it seemed like a good idea at the time. I don't think I even thought about it particularly consciously. ... She was much more sexually experienced than me. She knew exactly what was going to happen. I really didn't.

Q: Do you remember how you felt at the time, or afterwards?

A: Was that it? kind of thing. My uppermost feeling. I think I came very quickly, I don't normally have as much foreplay involved, and she seemed to enjoy herself, but I don't know how much that was due to me either. I suspect very little. It wasn't something I really thought was a sort of major cross roads in my life or anything, "Now I have lost my virginity, now I am a man" sort of thing. I don't think I ever had any of those sort of feelings.

We find a parallel to male acceptance of the knowing older women in the WRAP study of young women. Some young women, often after negative sexual experiences, employ the strategy of only having relationships with younger men, where they have more power to control both the sex and the relationship (Holland *et al.*, 1991).

The knowing older woman is acceptable, sought after, even if experiencing vulnerability may prove problematic.[13] The knowing female friend, with whom they can discuss the intricacies of relationships, and seek advice and comfort also figures widely in the experience of the young men in the sample. In this case she need not necessarily be sexually experienced herself, but can provide information about the physical aspects of women's bodies (including periods, a subject on which many of the young men required schooling), and emotional aspects of relationships from the woman's perspective. Mothers and older sisters could sometimes fulfil this function. The knowing younger woman is an altogether different matter.

(iv) The knowing woman: 'Slag' - the feared and fearsome reputation

As we have seen, having sexual experience puts a young woman in danger of acquiring a 'slack' reputation as a slag, as can expressing active sexual desires by being 'forward'. The fear of such a reputation can exercise strong control over a young woman's sexual experience and identity (Lees, 1986; Thomson and Scott, 1991; Holland *et al.*, 1990). For young men, the power of being able to attribute a negative reputation to the sexually knowing woman can counterbalance the fear of vulnerability in exposing themselves to her capacity for comparison and skill assessment. This strategy is related to the male model of masculinity and objectification of women, and we have seen some examples of how the attribution of experience to young women can enable this objectifying approach in the "bastard syndrome" discussed above. It is also related to the presence of peer pressure.

The following young man does seem to have been able to overcome the impact on his own behaviour of what he recognises as a double standard:

Q: Since women are changing do you think it's okay for the woman to make the first approach?
A: I think it would help a lot of men out if they did.
Q: You don't think they are though?
A: Some are. I think it helps a great deal if they do, I think it's just something born out of like what people think should happen. Women probably feel that they shouldn't really make the first move because the men are going to think something of them that they shouldn't do.
Q: You think they might think badly of them?
A: Yes I think that happens quite a bit, which is a shame really, because it's like the old thing that if the man makes the first move he's just looked at in a different light to what if the woman did the same thing.   [YM 24]

And this young man is quite happy for his own girlfriend to make the first moves, but it appears to be her age which makes it acceptable:

A: That's just due to an age gap, she's like twenty five so it doesn't bother me. It's actually nice for me for all the right reasons.

Perhaps he would not be quite so happy if his girlfriend was the same age.[14] Other young men who consider that it is hard for men to make the first move and would be helpful if girls did so, express more clearly contradictory views:

A: Like girls always expect blokes to make the first move, I think that's a pretty common thought and if they want to be equal then they should make the first move as well but they never do and that's fairly frustrating from a bloke's point of view.
Q: Then how might you feel about it a girl if a girl came on to you?

A: I always sit there and I always consider it to myself ... I would say yes, that would be all right ... [he is expressing this view rather doubtfully]

Q: It might be related to this slag thing, because they feel that if they make the first move the guy's going to think they want sex, they must be a slag, do you think that's the way it works out?

A: Yes, it would because if the girl made a big move on me I would just take it as a big come one, I would presume they wanted sex.   [YM 9]

Men who feel that a man has to prove himself, be a 'gladiator' are made vulnerable by the knowing woman, and might avoid getting definitive information about their performance:

A: I have never asked someone afterwards, was it good for you because if they said 'well, actually ...' I'd die.   [YM 21]

For the following young man the emphasis on male performance clearly puts women at an advantage as assessor of performance. He argues that

A: ...It's important for a man to feel he's a success sort of thing, whereas the woman - he can ask a woman what it was like and stuff like that, if he was good, but if he didn't give her an orgasm then he is a failure sort of thing ... I think it's more important for a man

Q: What, to feel successful?

A: Yes.

Q: Why is that then?

A: He has shown he is a dominant figure like whilst having sex, he has to be the one to - I don't know - feel successful at the end doesn't he?   [YM 10]

This conception of dominance and success in relation to sexual performance can threaten masculinity, since men then have to prove their prowess to women, as well as report it back to men:

Q: ...do you think that men are more nervous than women, or women more nervous than men?

A: I think men are more nervous than women because they are the ones that have got something to prove like, sort of thing, so I think like men have got to be a bit more nervous than women in a way.

Q: So in reality it is women who are in the more dominant position?

A: Yes, because they have got to like - they sort of like assess the

performance sort of thing, if you get what I mean, afterwards they
say I was lousy and something like that. The men have to prove to
them that they are capable of doing it with them.
....
Q: Is there a sort of feeling do you think amongst men to think they have
to be good at sex?
A: I think so yes, especially if you have seen the girl about and stuff like
that, and like you know she is going to open her mouth to everyone else
if you are not good, so yes, you have to perform quite well if you know
the girl like, and you have seen her about.
Q: Does that make you quite nervous thinking you have to perform quite
well?
A: Sometimes it does.   [YM 10]

This need to be 'good at sex' distances young men from perceiving
masculinity in terms of possible relationships. It feeds into a competitive and
limited conception of male sexuality in which men can become sexually
'successful', while cutting themselves off from emotional dependence. The
gladiator then wields a two edged sword - proving his manhood to himself and
his peers, while cutting the ground from beneath himself.

CONCLUSION: VULNERABILITY AND POWER

The social construction of sexuality, viewed from the accounts of these young
men, gives a different perspective on sexual encounters from those of young
women. Young men were clearly aware that in entering into the negotiation of
sexual encounters they were laying themselves open to the possibility of failure.
Their strategies for dealing with their potential vulnerability reproduce and
reinforce the exercise of male power over women. Young men do not need to
have any intention, nor even any awareness, of subordinating women in order
to exercise power over them. Their struggles to be successfully masculine, to
emerge as young gladiators rather than as wimps, involve them in defining their
sexuality in terms of male needs, male desires and male satisfactions, rather than
in terms that might acknowledge and engage with female sexuality.

The way in which this competition for masculinity is played out,
protects men from acknowledging a subtext of men's fears of an
independent female sexuality. Fear is not generally expressed directly
in the transcripts, but is implied obliquely in the defensive strategies
with which young men protect their masculinity from the power of
women's desires, and from dependence on women. Where young men
resist the pressures of masculinity by developing relationships with

women which put their masculinity at risk, they are still aware of, and measured against the young gladiators. As they get older, a possible strategy is to become family men, providers and household heads with dependants, allowing them both to develop relationships, and to be masculine. This is, however, an unstable and risky strategy, as levels of domestic violence, divorce and the break-up of partnerships indicate. For younger men, their masculinity is closely identified with their sexuality, and the need to differentiate themselves from the feminine.

Whether or not individual young men emerge successfully into hegemonic masculinity, the social processes which constitute becoming a man shore up the enormous strength of men's sexual domination of women. In these processes men can certainly suffer pain, humiliation, loss, ridicule and rejection, yet both wimps and gladiators exercise power over women through their acquisition of masculinity. As we have argued elsewhere (Holland *et al.* 1992a) young women, in producing themselves as feminine, enable men to exercise power over them. While it is possible for both men and women to resist the pressures of masculinity and femininity, in practice few manage such resistance (for example 'coming out' as gay while still at school) and to resist masculinity is to fail as a man. Men are then in a contradictory situation in which they suffer from being socially pressured into a narrow and constraining conception of masculine sexuality, but they also benefit from social arrangements which systematically privilege the male over the female.

NOTES

1   We are grateful for the contributions of Rachel Thomson and Tim Rhodes to this paper. This is a first approach to the data on young men's sexuality, and some of the ideas which we have not had space to develop here will be developed by the WRAP/MRAP team in later publications.

2   We agree with the view that there is no natural male sex drive.

3   The Women, Risk and AIDS Project study of young women was staffed by the authors and Sue Scott, now at the University of Stirling, and Rachel Thomson, now coordinating the Sex Education Forum of the National Children's Bureau, working collectively, and was financed by a two year grant from the ESRC. Additional funding was contributed by the Department of Health, and Goldsmiths' College Research Fund. Valuable assistance has been given by Jane Preston, Polly Radcliffe and Janet Ransom. WRAP used a purposive sample to interview 150 young women in depth between 1988 and 1990. A pre-selection questionnaire (completed by 500 young women) provided a statistical profile of a large (non-random) sample. From this sample we drew the purposive sample on the basis of the variables of age, ethnicity, power/socio-economic class, education and sexual activity.

4   The Leverhulme Trust gave a one year grant for this comparative study, and Tim Rhodes, now at the Centre for Research on Drugs and Health Behaviour, was a team member on this project. The study included interviews with 15 advisors on sexuality to young people. A pre-selection questionnaire was also used in this project which gave additional statistical data on 250 young men.

5   The relationship between the exercise and experience of power in a heterosexual sexual encounter and the broad societal institutionalisation of male power remains to be explained.

6   See Appendix 2 for a brief biographical description of the young men quoted in this paper.

7   This joking discourse, expressing masculine identity and reinforcing how young men should and should not define their own identities occurs in a number of settings, including the school and the family (see below).

8   Some of the young men we talked to had had sexual experiences with men, but in this paper we are focusing on heterosexual masculinity.

9   Many would say that was in fact what they wanted.

10   Further vulnerability is created for many young men in that they do not believe in, or agree with, the male model of sexuality by which they are judged.

11   See Holland *et al.* (1991) for an appropriated female form of this instrumental model.

12   Daniel Wight found this response in his sample of 19 year old men (personal communication).

13   Kelly *et al.* (1991:7), in their study of child abuse reported by 1200 16-21 year olds, found 3 cases of older women sexualising relationships with young men, but the young men did not experience these as victimising. The same was true in the one case of female on male child sexual abuse reported in our data. See also Fromuth and Burkhart (1987).

14   There is a complex interplay of factors from which power can be derived - age, knowledge, gender, 'race' - which can lead to a delicate balance of relational power. In this case the young man has focused on differential age as legitimising a shift in gendered power.

REFERENCES

Aggleton, P. (Ed.) (1992) *Young People and HIV/AIDS; Papers from an ESRC Sponsored Seminar on Young People and HIV/AIDS Social Research*, Swindon: ESRC with HEA and Goldsmiths' College
Allen, I. (1987) *Education in sex and personal relationships*, PSI Report No. 665.
Brittan, A. (1989) *Masculinity and power*, Oxford: Blackwell.
Brod, H. (Ed.) (1987) *The making of masculinities*, Boston: Allen & Unwin.
Carrigan, T., Connell, R. W. & Lee, J. (1985) Toward a new sociology of masculinity, *Theory and Society*, 14, (5), 551-604.
Chapman, R. & Rutherford, J. (Eds.) (1988) *Male order: Unwrapping masculinity*, London: Lawrence & Wishart.
Clatterbaugh, K. (1990) *Contemporary perspectives on masculinity: Men, women and politics in modern society*, Boulder, Colorado: Westview Press.
Curry, C. (1990) Young people in independent schools, sexual behaviour and AIDS. In Aggleton, P., Davies, P., an Hart, G. (Eds.), *AIDS: Individual, cultural and policy dimensions*, Lewes: Falmer Press
Fromuth, M. and Burkhart, B. (1987) Childhood sexual victimisation among college men: definitional and methodological issues, *Violence and victims*, 2, (4), 533-542.
Hall, L. (1991) *Hidden anxieties: Male sexuality 1900-1950*, Cambridge: Polity.
Hearn, J. & Morgan, D. (Eds.) (1990) *Men, masculinities and social theory*, London: Unwin Hyman.
Holland, J., Ramazanoglu, C., Scott, S., Sharpe, S. & Thomson, R. (1990) *'Don't die of ignorance' I nearly died of embarrassment: Condoms in context*, London: the Tufnell Press.
Holland, J., Ramazanoglu, C., Scott, S., Sharpe, S. & Thomson, R. (1992a) Pressure, resistance, empowerment: Young women and the negotiation of safer sex. In P. Aggleton, P. Davies and G. Hart (Eds.), *AIDS: Rights, Risk and Reason* London: Falmer Press.
Holland, J., Ramazanoglu, C., Sharpe, S. & Thomson, R. (1992b) 'Power and desire: the embodiment of female sexuality' paper given to the *Alice in Wonderland Conference on Girls and Girlhood: Transitions and Dilemmas*, Amsterdam.
Holland, J., Ramazanoglu, C., Sharpe, S. and Thomson, R. (1992c) Pleasure, pressure and power: Some contradictions of gendered sexuality, *Sociological Review*, 40 (4) 645-674
Hollway, W. (1984) Women's power in heterosexual sex, *Women's Studies International Forum*, 7, 63-8.

Ingham, R., Woodcock, A. and Stenner, K. (1991) 'Getting to know you ... young people's knowledge of their partners at first intercourse,' *Journal of Community and Applied Social Psychology* 1.

Kelly, L., Regan, L., Burton, S. (1991) *An exploratory study of the prevalence of sexual abuse in a sample of 16-21 year olds,* Child Abuse Studies Unit, Polytechnic of North London, 62-66 Ladbroke House, Highbury Grove, London N5 2AD

Kent, V., Davies, M., Deverell, K. and Gottesman, S. (1990) 'Social interaction routines involved in heterosexual encounters: prelude to first intercourse'. Paper presented at the *Fourth Conference on the Social Aspects of AIDS*, London.

Kimmel, M. S. (Ed.) (1987) *Changing men: New directions in research on men and masculinity*, Newbury Park, California: Sage.

Lees, S. (1986) *Losing out: Sexuality and adolescent girls*, London: Hutchinson.

Litewka, J. (1977) "The socialised penis" in Snodgrass, J. (Ed.) *For men against sexism*, Albion, Ca: Times Change Press.

Mahoney, P. (1985) *Schools for the boys? Co-education reassessed*, London: Hutchinson and The Explorations in Feminism Collective.

Morgan, D. (1981). Men, masculinity and the process of sociological enquiry. In Helen Roberts (Ed.), *Doing feminist research*, London: Routledge & Kegan Paul.

Nix, L.M., Pasteur, A.B., Servance, M.A. (1988) 'A focus group study of sexually active black male teenagers'. *Adolescence*. 23, 91: 741-743.

Pleck, J. H, Sonenstein, F.L. and Swain, S.O. (1988) 'Adolescent males' sexual behaviour and contraceptive use: implications for male responsibility'. *Journal of Adolescent Research*. 3, 3-4

Ramazanoglu, C. (1992) 'What can you do with a man? Feminism and the critical appraisal of masculinity', *Women's Studies International Forum* 15, 3:339-50.

Segal, L. (1990) *Slow motion*, London: Virago.

Seidler, V. J. (1989) *Rediscovering masculinity: reason, language and sexuality*, London: Routledge.

Seidler, V. J. (1991a) *Recreating sexual politics: men, feminism and politics*, London: Routledge.

Seidler, V. J. (Ed.) (1991b) *The Achilles heel reader: men, sexual politics and socialism*, London: Routledge.

Spencer, B. (1984) 'Young men: their attitudes towards sexuality and birth control', *British Journal of Family Planning*. 10: 13-19.

Thompson, S. (1990) 'Putting a big thing into a little hole: teenage girls' accounts of sexual initiation,' *The Journal of Sex Research* 27, 3:341-361.

Thomson, R. and Scott, S. (1991) *Learning about sex: Young women and the social construction of sexual identity*. London: the Tufnell Press (Reprinted 1992).

Tiefer, L. (1987) In pursuit of the perfect penis: The medicalisation of male sexuality. In Michael S. Kimmel (Ed.), *Changing men: New directions in research on men and masculinity*, Newbury Park, California: Sage.

Tolson, A. (1977) *The limits of masculinity*, London: Tavistock.

Wight, D. (1993) 'Constraints or cognition: Factors affecting young men's practice of safer heterosexual sex'. In Aggleton, P., Davies, P., and Hart, G. (eds.) *AIDS: The Second Decade*, London: Falmer.

Wight, D. (1992) 'Boys' thoughts and talk about sex in a working class locality or Glasgow' (Unpublished paper) 6 Lilybank Gdns, Glasgow G12 8QQ: Medical Sociology Unit.

Wight, D. (1990). The impact of HIV/AIDS on young people's sexual behaviour in Britain: a literature review, 6 Lilybank Gdns, Glasgow G12 8QQ: Medical Sociology Unit.

Wood, J. (1987) 'Groping towards sexism: boys' sex talk.' In G. Weiner and M. Arnot *Gender Under Scrutiny: New Inquiries in Education*, London: Unwin Hyman.

Woodcock, A., Stenner, K, and Ingham, R. (1992) 'Young people talking about HIV and AIDS: interpretations of personal risk and infection' *Health Education Research: Theory and Practice.*

APPENDIX 1:

Statistical description of sample of young men and young women

Table 1: Class distribution of the sample of young women (WRAP)

Age	mc n	mc %	lmc n	lmc %	tot mc n	tot mc %	uwc n	uwc %	wc n	wc %	tot wc n	tot wc %	%
1	10	17	10	17	20	34	6	10	33	56	39	66	59
2	16	36	12	27	28	64	1	2	15	34	16	36	44
3	13	29	8	18	26	58	6	13	18	40	24	53	45
Tots	39	26	30	20	69	47	13	9	66	45	79	53	148

Table 2: Class distribution of the sample of young men (MRAP)

Age	mc n	mc %	lmc n	lmc %	tot mc n	tot mc %	uwc n	uwc %	wc n	wc %	tot wc n	tot wc %	%
1	5	21	3	13	8	35	3	13	12	52	15	6	23
2	6	40	2	13	8	53	0	0	7	47	7	47	15
3	4	50	1		5	68	1		2	25	3	38	8
Tots	15	33	6	13	21	46	4	9	21	46	25	54	46

Table 3: Sexual activity in the samples
(a)   Sexually active by age: Young women

	sa	not sa	
Age 1	39 (66%)	20 (34%)	59
Age 2	38 (86%)	6 (14%)	44
Age 3	44 (98%)	1 (2%)	45
Tots	121 (82%)	27 (18%)	148

(b)   Sexually active by age: Young men

	sa	not sa	
Age 1	18 (78%)	5 22%)	23
Age 2	15(100%)	0 (0%)	15
Age 3	7 (88%)	1 (12%)	8
Tots	40 (87%)	6 (13%)	46

(c)   Average age of first sex

	male	female
Age 1	12.82	14.07
Age 2	12.93	15.57
Age 3	13.85	16.27
Tot	13.05	15.4

(d)   Average number of partners

		male	female
Age 1			
	Casual with intercourse	2.94	0.70
	Steady with intercourse	0.83	0.90
Age 2			
	Casual with intercourse	1.66	1.20
	Steady with intercourse	2.66	1.50
Age 3			
	Casual with intercourse	4.71	5.02
	Steady with intercourse	2.57	2.41
Tots	Casual with intercourse	2.78	2.43
	Steady with intercourse	1.66	1.64

Key:				
	Age 1:	16-17,11	mc	middle class
	Age 2:	18-19,11	wc	working class
	Age 3:	20-21,11	lmc/wc	lower mc/wc
	sa: Sexually active		umc/wc	upper mc/wc

APPENDIX 2

Short Biographies:

YM1   Aged 19. Lives with four friends. Studying for a degree at university.
YM2   Aged 21. Lives with friends in student house. Studying for a degree at university
YM3   Aged 19. Lives at home with parents and older brother. Studying for HND at college.
YM4   Aged 17. Lives at home with parents and two older brothers. Studying for A levels at school (or just finished?)
YM5   Aged 20. Lives with friends. Studying for a degree at polytechnic.
YM6   Aged 16. Lives at home with parents, brother and sister.
YM7   Aged 19. Lives with father and younger brother. Works as engineer.
YM8   Aged 17. Lives at home with mother. At school studying for A levels.
YM9   Aged 16. Lives at home with parents , two brothers and sister.Studying A levels at sixth form college.
YM10 Aged 16. Lives at home with parents and brothers. Attending training agency; looking for youth training course.
YM11 Aged 19. Lives at home with father and younger brother. About to start a degree at university after having a year off.
YM12 Aged 18. Lives at home with parents and younger brother. Taking a YTS course in theatre studies..
YM13 Aged 20. Lives at home with father. Doing an apprenticeship and taking day release in car mechanics.
YM14 Aged 19. Lives at home with mother and sister. At college, doing a Btec course.
YM15 Aged 17. Lives at home with mother and three brothers and three sisters. At sixth form college, studying for A levels.
YM16 Aged 16. Lives at home with father and stepmother. Attending training agency, wants to be a motor mechanic.
YM17 Aged 20. Lives at home with parents and younger brother. Works as an engineer.
YM18 Aged 21. Lives on his own. studying for a degree at university.
YM19 Aged 18. Lives at home with mother and older brother and younger sister. Works nights replacing stock in a store.
YM20 Aged 17. Lives at home with parents. Attending training agency, wants to be a motor mechanic.
YM21 Aged 17. Lives at home with mother, stepfather, stepbrother and sister. At school studying for A levels.
YM22 Aged 18. Lives at home with parents and two sisters. At school studying GCSE and A level in sixth form.
YM23 Aged 19. Lives at home with parents. Works as an engineer; at college studying City and Guilds on day release.
YM24 Aged 19. Lives at home with parents. Just left school after taking A levels; looking for advertising job.
YM25 Aged 18. Lives at home with mother. Studying for Btec.
YW14 Aged 21. Lives alone in a flat. Works as a nursery nurse.

Sexuality and ethnicity: Variations in young women's sexual knowledge and practice
Janet Holland

In this paper the author describes the sample of 150 young women who took part in the WRAP study, focusing on similarities and differences between young women from different broad ethnic groups - white, African-Caribbean, and Asian. We discuss their experience and knowledge of sex education, AIDS and AIDS education, and consider family and cultural influences on sexual behaviour. Their perceptions of men, women and sexual relationships, and understanding of risk and safety in sexual encounters are examined. Despite differences in class, cultural, religious and educational background there was perhaps a surprising degree of similarity in the young women's responses. The paper concludes by drawing out implications of the findings for policy and practice.

210 x 150 mm	44pp	1993
ISBN 1 872767 85 0	Paperback	£3.50

Pressured pleasure: Young women and the negotiation of sexual boundaries
Janet Holland, Caroline Ramazanoglu, Sue Sharpe & Rachel Thomson

Women develop and live their sexuality through an interrelated range of pressures; personal, social, physical. The authors examine the continuum of pressure, from social expectation to male physical violence, which shapes women's sexuality, sexual identity and sexual health. They describe and illustrate the boundaries of sexual pressure and violence, and the degree to which women are able to negotiate these boundaries. Modes of resistance and types of experience, both negative and positive, which can enable young women to take control over their own sexuality and sexual experienceare examined.

210 x 150 mm	30pp	1992
ISBN 1 872767 80 X	Paperback	£3.50

Pressure, resistance, empowerment: Young women and the negotiation of safer sex
Janet Holland, Caroline Ramazanoglu, Sue Scott, Sue Sharpe & Rachel Thomson

We reflect here on the sexual politics of safer sex by considering ways in which young women can become empowered in sexual encounters. Selected case studies illustrate difficulties which young women face in taking control of their sexuality and sexual experience. Some become assertive individuals, but their experiences demonstrate that empowerment for women must be a collective project shifting the balance of power between men and women throughout society.

210 x 150 mm	30pp	1991
ISBN 1 872767 75 3	Paperback	£3.00

Learning about sex: young women and the social construction of sexual identity
Rachel Thomson & Sue Scott

Sex education is an interactive process in which young women actively engage with, resist and accommodate a range of contradictory messages and models. In this paper the way young women experience 'learning about sex' related to their sexual practice and expectations of sexual pleasure is examined. Available models of female sexuality and influences and information sources including the home, peer groups, popular culture and experience are discussed. Understanding the social construction of sexual identity has important implications for the negotiation of safe sex.

| 210 X 150 mm | 55 pp | 1992 (rev) |
| ISBN 1 872767 70 2 | Paperback | £3.50 |

'Don't die of ignorance' - I nearly died of embarrassment: Condoms in context
Janet Holland, Caroline Ramazanoglu, Sue Scott, Sue Sharpe, and Rachel Thomson

Negotiation of sexual encounters is a complex process with many different outcomes. In this paper the relationship between knowledge of risk and safer sex practices is examined through an analysis of young women's reported experience of condom use, from which it is clear that gendered power relations construct and constrain the choices open to young women.

| 210 X 150 mm | 30 pp | 1990 |
| ISBN 1 872767 50 8 | Paperback | £3.00 |

Sex, risk and danger: AIDS education policy and young women's sexuality
Janet Holland, Caroline Ramazanoglu and Sue Scott

The authors review the history of the AIDS epidemic in medical science, social research and public policy, highlighting the way in which women have been perceived and represented in that process. AIDS education aimed at young heterosexuals is evaluated in the light of the findings of an investigation of the sexual knowledge and practice of a group of young women.

| 210 X 150 mm | 30 pp | 1990 |
| ISBN 1 872767 55 9 | Paperback | £3.00 |

Researching sexuality in the light of AIDS: Historical and methodological issues
Rachel Thomson and Sue Scott

The methodological implications of treating sexuality as a socially constructed subject are explored in relation to the findings of the WRAP study of young women's sexuality.

210 X 150 mm	26 pp	1990
ISBN 1 872767 65 6	Paperback	£3.00

Methods of working as a research team
Caroline Ramazanoglu

The author examines problems of making explicit the relationship between theory construction and data production; of hierarchical relationships within the team; of power in the research process; of the negotiation of meanings both with informants and within the research team; of validity and interpretation of qualitative data; and of the place of trust and emotion in the research process.

210 X 150 mm	30 pp	1990
ISBN 1 872767 60 5	Paperback	£3.00

the Tufnell Press
47 Dalmeny Road,
London, N7 0DY

ORDER FORM

Please send me the following:

	Price	Quantity	Total

Postage outside UK £1.00 per copy ⎯⎯⎯

Total amount enclosed ⎯⎯⎯

Please make cheques payable to the Tufnell Press

NAME   _____

ADDRESS

                 _____

                 _____

                 _____   W9/1993

Women, Risk, and AIDS Project

Men, Risk, and AIDS Project

Young people, sexuality and the limitation of AIDS

The WRAP and MRAP studies have explored the sexual practices, beliefs and understanding of young women and men in London and Manchester. Using a range of research methods, young people aged between 16 and 21 have been studied, producing a detailed description and analysis of what they know about sexuality and AIDS, the ideas which they have about risk, danger and control in sexual encounters, how and why they behave as they do in sexual relationships, and what factors are likely to constrain or encourage change in their behaviour. Practical and policy implications of the findings have been drawn out in the working paper series.

The WRAP/MRAP team

Janet Holland,	*Senior Research Officer, Institute of Education, London*
Caroline Ramazanoglu,	*Senior Lecturer, Goldsmiths College, London*
Sue Scott,	*Senior Lecturer, University of Stirling*
Sue Sharpe,	*Consultant Researcher, London*
Rachel Thomson,	*Consultant Researcher, London*
Tim Rhodes,	*Research Fellow, Centre for Research on Drugs and Health Behaviour*

Descriptions of the WRAP Papers may be found at the back of this book.

Wimp or gladiator
Contradictions in acquiring masculine sexuality